Land and Water

STUDENT ACTIVITY BOOK

SCIENCE AND TECHNOLOGY FOR CHILDREN™

NATIONAL SCIENCE RESOURCES CENTER
Smithsonian Institution • National Academy of Sciences
Arts and Industries Building, Room 1201
Washington, DC 20560

NSRC

The National Science Resources Center is operated by the Smithsonian Institution and the National Academy of Sciences to improve the teaching of science in the nation's schools. The NSRC collects and disseminates information about exemplary teaching resources, develops and disseminates curriculum materials, and sponsors outreach activities, specifically in the areas of leadership development and technical assistance, to help school districts develop and sustain hands-on science programs.

STC Project Supporters

National Science Foundation
Smithsonian Institution
U.S. Department of Defense
U.S. Department of Education
John D. and Catherine T. MacArthur Foundation
The Dow Chemical Company Foundation
E. I. du Pont de Nemours & Company
Amoco Foundation, Inc.
Hewlett-Packard Company
Smithsonian Institution Educational Outreach Fund
Smithsonian Women's Committee

This project was supported, in part,
by the
National Science Foundation
Opinions expressed are those of the authors
and not necessarily those of the Foundation

Published by Carolina Biological Supply Company, 2700 York Road, Burlington, NC 27215.
Call toll free 800-334-5551.

This material is based upon work supported by the National Science Foundation under Grant No. ESI-9252947. Any opinions, findings, and conclusions or recommendations expressed in this material are those of the author(s) and do not necessarily reflect the views of the National Science Foundation.

CB787459809

♻ Printed on recycled paper.

Contents

Thinking about Land and Water

Think and Wonder

What do you know about land and water? What would you like to find out? Today, you will think about these things. You will also look at some photos of land and water. What observations can you make?

Materials

For you
　　1　science notebook

For you and your partner
　　1　*Land and Water* Student Activity Book

For you and your group
　　4　photo cards (numbered 1, 2, 3, and 4)

Find Out for Yourself

1. Your teacher will give you a science notebook. Write today's date on the first page.

2. What do you know about land and water? Take a few minutes to write your ideas in your science notebook.

3. Now share some of these ideas with the class. Your teacher will record them on a list.

4. What would you like to find out about land and water? Write some thoughts in your science notebook. Then share your ideas and questions with the class.

5. Which of the ideas your teacher has recorded are about water? Which are about land? Which are about both?

6. Your teacher will give your group four photo cards. Look at them with your group. Pick two cards to write about. Record the numbers of the two photo cards in your notebook. Then write your observations about each photo card.

7. Flip the photo cards over. Copy the questions on the back of each photo card into your notebook. Put the card number next to each question. Then answer the questions.

8. When you are finished writing, share your answers with the class.

9. Land and water affect each other in many ways. How could you study them in the classroom? In the next lesson, you will build a model to help you do this.

Ideas to Explore

1. Observe the land around your home or school. How has the land been affected by flowing water? Write your thoughts on paper. Use lots of "describing" words. Trade your writing with a classmate. Then draw a picture of your classmate's writing.

2. People often travel to interesting places and see unusual landforms. Ask your parents or other adults about landforms they have seen while on vacation. Share their answers with the class. Your teacher can help you record, on a graph, the places and how many of the people you surveyed have visited them. You can also try to find the places on a map.

Figure 1-1

Sample vacation survey of landforms

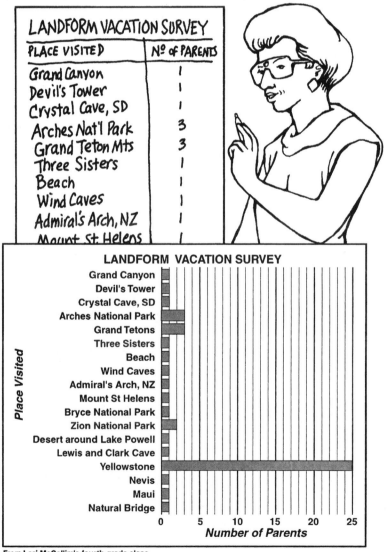

From Lori McCollim's fourth-grade class,
Willson Science and Technology School,
Bozeman, MT

The Water Cycle: Modeling Land and Water

Think and Wonder

You may have made a model car or a model of a house out of blocks. Today, you will make a model of land and water on earth. Then you will use the model to learn about the water cycle. You will get to read about the water cycle, too.

Materials

For you
  1 science notebook

Stream table materials for you and your group
  *1 plastic box, lid, and stopper
  *1 storage container with the following items:
       *1 small pad
       *1 large pad
       *1 plastic spreader
       *1 spoon
       *1 ruler
       *2 hand lenses
       *1 bucket

Other materials for you and your group
  1 soda bottle of warm water
  1 piece of plastic wrap
  1 large rubber band
  1 ice pack

*These stream table materials are used in almost every lesson. Beginning in Lesson 3, you will not see each of these items listed individually. Instead, you will just see the words "stream table materials" in your list.

Find Out for Yourself

1. Today, you will build a model. But first, talk about these questions with the class:

   - What models have you seen or made?

   - How does the size of a model compare with that of the actual object?

   - How do the features of the model compare with those of the actual object?

   - What are some examples of models scientists might use?

   - Why do you think scientists use models?

2. Look at the class list from Lesson 1. Now think about what a "water cycle" might be. What items on the list have to do with the water cycle? Share your thoughts with the class.

3. Look at the box of soil, bottle of water, and plastic wrap your teacher has on display. How could you use these materials to model the water cycle on earth?

4. Look at the **Student Instructions for Modeling the Water Cycle** on pgs. 9–10. Read along as your teacher goes over them.

5. Help your group pick up its materials. You need one box of soil, one storage container of materials, one bottle of water, one sheet of plastic, and one rubber band. You can pick up the ice pack later, when you are ready to use it.

6. Now help your group set up the model. Use the instructions on pgs. 9–10.

7. What observations did you make about the water cycle? Share your thoughts with the class.

8. Look at Figure 2-1. What part of the illustration is like your ice pack?

9. In your notebook, write the answers to these questions:

   - After what you observed in the lesson, what do you know about rain?

   - What do you know about how water meets land?

10. Talk with the class about the ideas you wrote down.

11. Be sure to clean up. Here's what you need to do:

   - Remove the rubber band and plastic.

   - Take out the stopper. Drain the water from the model into the bucket.

   - Carefully tilt the plastic box to drain any extra water into the catch bucket (see Figure 2-2).

   - Put the stopper back in the drain hole from inside the box.

   - Stack the boxes without their lids. Your teacher can show you how.

   - Your teacher can tell you where to put the other materials. If the pads are dry, fold them and put them in your group's storage container. If they are wet, lay them flat to dry.

Figure 2-1

A model of land,
water, and the
water cycle

Figure 2-2

Tilting the
plastic box

12. Now read "Tapping into the Water Cycle" on pgs. 11–14. Then write down one way people collect water for daily use.

Ideas to Explore

1. Do today's investigation again. This time use a flashlight. Shine it on the lake you modeled in your stream table. What happens? Why? What does the flashlight represent?

2. Do solids evaporate? Find out by putting a pan of salt water in the sun. Write down your observations over time. What happens? Why?

3. Could you make a model of the water cycle using materials different from the ones in today's lesson? Give it a try!

4. You know that water can change from a liquid to a gas. At what temperature does this happen? (Think about both Celsius and Fahrenheit.) At what temperature does water change from a liquid to a solid? Do some research to find out.

5. Does the water cycle happen in your home? What about outdoors? Take a look and write about your observations. You may want to write a poem.

Student Instructions for Modeling the Water Cycle

1. Cover your work space with the large absorbent pad. Make sure the absorbent side faces up and the plastic side is down.

2. Place the small absorbent pad on the floor so the absorbent side faces up.

3. Place the clear plastic box of soil on the large absorbent pad. Remove the lid.

4. Make certain the rubber stopper is pushed tightly into the drain hole from inside the box.

5. Mix the soil in the box with the plastic spreader.

6. With the spreader, "bulldoze" the soil. Push the soil away from the drain hole toward the opposite end of the box, as shown in the picture.

7. Now create a lake in your model. Pour the warm water into the box. *Do not pour the water on the soil.*

8. Cover your land and water model (the plastic box) with plastic wrap. Fasten the plastic with a large rubber band, as shown in the picture.

9. Get a frozen ice pack from your teacher.

10. Place the ice pack on the plastic so it is above the land, as shown in the picture. Do not touch the ice pack during the next five minutes.

11. What do you think will happen in the model? While you are waiting, discuss your predictions within your group. Record your predictions in your notebook.

12. After five or more minutes, remove the ice pack from the plastic. Look at the plastic. Discuss your observations within your group. Record your observations in your notebook.

13. Tap gently on the plastic where you placed the ice pack. Record your observations.

Reading Selection

Tapping into the Water Cycle

Turn on a faucet and what happens? Out comes fresh, clean water. But where does this water come from and why doesn't it ever run out?

Think about all the water on earth. You can find it in lakes, streams, and oceans. Some of it is frozen on snow-capped mountains. Other water is hidden underground. Of all the water on earth, only a small amount can be used for drinking.

Oceans 97.2%

Fresh water 2.8%

Icecaps and glaciers

Ground water

Water in atmosphere

Surface water (lakes, rivers, streams)

Water on earth

What Goes Around Comes Around

Water is constantly moving. This is because of the **water cycle.** As the sun heats the earth, water changes to a gas. Minerals, such as salt, and other particles are left behind. The gas, called **water vapor,** rises high into the cold air and clings to particles of dust. The cold air turns the gas back into water droplets. Many of these droplets combine to form clouds. Eventually the clouds gather more water than they can hold. Then the water falls back to earth as rain, snow, sleet, or hail. In a continuous cycle, water moves out of the oceans, into the atmosphere, and back down to earth.

The water cycle is vital to life on earth. Without it, all of the world's water would end up in the oceans and stay there forever. Rain would not fall to the earth. Plants could not live. Streams would dry up. Ponds would empty. The land would become a lifeless desert. And your faucet would run dry.

Condensation

Precipitation

Transpiration

Surface runoff

Evaporation

Water table

Ground water

The water cycle

Rainwater keeps our lakes, streams, and land filled with water. It supplies our drinking water. But rainwater does not fall evenly over the earth. In fact, some areas get almost no rain at all. People all over the world have found clever ways to collect and store water. How do they do it? Let's visit a few places and see.

Collecting Rainfall for Year-Round Use

In the southwestern United States, weeks and often months go by without rain. **Droughts,** or long periods without rain, are common. Droughts cause crops to fail. Streams flowing over the dense clay soil gradually dry up.

To deal with this problem, citizens in Austin, Texas, have created a way to collect rainfall they can use all year long—they use their roofs! Outside one family's house, two 32,000-liter (8,500-gallon) tanks sit inside a large shed with a tin roof. When it rains, rainwater runs down the tin roof into the tanks below. Special lights in the tanks kill bacteria in the water. Water tests make certain the water is pure and clean. Then pipes carry the collected rainwater to different parts of the house. Even the downspouts along the edge of the house are set up to collect rainwater. This water can be used for appliances and outdoor use. A rainwater collection system like this one can supply a family with 190 liters (50 gallons) of water a day for 11 months!

Melting Rivers of Ice

In the mountains of the northwestern United States and Canada, most of the year is very cold. Water stays frozen as snow or rivers of

Rainwater collection system

ice, known as **glaciers.** But people have found ways to tap into these frozen water sources. How? During the warm and dry summer months, there is little rainfall. As the sun beats down, the ice and snow begin to melt. People collect and use the meltwater for drinking, bathing, and other uses in the home. Businesses use the water to run machines. And farmers use the water to irrigate their crops. People store the extra water for the winter months.

Net for collecting water from fog

Chile Today—Foggy All the Time!

Imagine a place where there is always fog, but it never rains! In Chungungo, a rural town in Chile, high in the Andes mountains in South America, water is scarce. Until recently, the only way for people to get water was to truck it from a village over 13 miles away on a dirt road. Most villagers could buy only 15 liters (4 gallons) of water a day. In the United States, each person uses an average of 350 liters (about 90 gallons) a day!

To solve this water shortage, scientists created a system that collects fresh water from fog. They lined up 75 enormous plastic nets on the mountain. Each net is the size of eight queen-sized beds. Particles of water from the fog collect in the triangular-shaped holes in the nets.

Over 10,000 particles of fog must combine to make one single drop of water. Yet each net collects over 152 liters (40 gallons) of water a day! A solar-powered system puts chlorine in the water. This makes the water safe to drink. In one day, the entire system of nets can collect 11,400 liters (3,000 gallons) of water—all from fog! This is enough water for one day for each of the town's 330 people.

Because of the water cycle, water can be used again and again. But clean drinking water is not easy to find everywhere on earth. Sometimes we take clean water for granted.

We forget that water must be shared by many people. Find out how much water you use each day. How could you cut back on the amount you use? Turn off your water and see.

Keep track of your daily water usage

Activity	Amount of Water Used	Number of Times (✔)	Total Water Used
			_____ liters (_____ gal)
Brushing teeth (without letting water run)	1 liter (¼ gal)		_____ liters (_____ gal)
Taking a shower	114 liters (30 gal)		_____ liters (_____ gal)
Flushing the toilet	6 liters (1½ gal)		_____ liters (_____ gal)
Drinking a glass of water	0.24 liter (8 oz or 1/16 gal)		_____ liters (_____ gal)
Taking a bath	152 liters (40 gal)		_____ liters (_____ gal)
Washing hands	1 liter (¼ gal)		_____ liters (_____ gal)
Washing dishes by hand	38 liters (10 gal)		_____ liters (_____ gal)

How much water do you use in one day?

Modeling Rain on Land

Think and Wonder

You have probably been caught in the rain without an umbrella. You know what happens to you. But have you ever wondered how rainfall affects the land? Where does the rain go? How does it change the land? Let's use our model and find out.

Materials

For you
   1   science notebook

For you and your group
       *Stream table materials
   1   sprinkler head
   1   soda bottle of water

* These are the materials you used in Lesson 2. They include the clear plastic box of soil and the storage container of materials. Together, they will be called "stream table materials" from now on.

Find Out for Yourself

1. Help the class remember what you observed in the last lesson about the water cycle.

2. Why do you think it might be important to work in groups? Discuss this with the class.

3. Your teacher will show you a soda bottle. What do you think the sprinkler head on the bottle could model in this lesson? Discuss your ideas with the class.

4. Help your group get its materials.

5. Today, you will rebuild your land model. Read along as your teacher goes over these steps:

   ■ As you did in Lesson 2, cover your work space with the large pad so the absorbent side faces up. Place the small pad on the floor so the absorbent side faces up.

- Place the clear plastic box of soil on top of the large absorbent pad.

- Make certain the rubber stopper is pushed tightly into the hole from the inside of the box.

- With the plastic spreader, mix the soil in the box.

- Use the plastic spreader to push the soil away from the hole toward the opposite end of the box, just as you did in Lesson 2. Bulldoze the soil into a single block that is about 20 cm (8 in) long. Smooth the surface of the soil with the plastic spreader.

- Now use the plastic spreader to create a gentle slope in the soil. It should be about 5 cm (2 in) deep at the far end and about 4.5 cm (1¾ in) at the end nearest the hole. This will prevent water from backing up on the soil.

- Again using the plastic spreader, create a vertical cliff at the edge of the soil, as shown in Figure 3-1.

Figure 3-1

*Sloped land
with cliff*

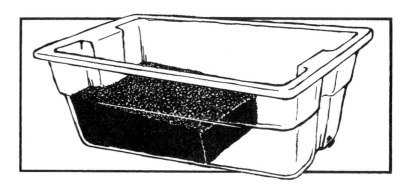

6. Why is it important to bulldoze the soil in the same way during each investigation? What do we mean by a "fair test?" Share your thoughts with the class.

7. During your investigation, water may run off the land. Look at Figure 3-2 while your teacher explains how to catch the runoff.

8. Watch as a classmate shows how to use the sprinkling bottle.

9. Start your group's investigation. Remember to use a bucket to catch the runoff. Also, do not touch the soil after you have begun raining on the land.

10. Take a look at the land models of the other groups.

11. Think about how your land model changed during the investigation. Answer these questions with the class. Point to places in your model that support your answers.

- What happened to the land as it rained? Why do you think this happened?

- What happened to the rainwater as it hit the land?

- Where did the water go?

Figure 3-2

*Catching the
runoff*

Student
"raining"
on soil

Water
draining
out of
hole into
catch bucket

Absorbent
pad

- Compare the water in the bucket with the water you rained on the land. How are they different? Can you explain why?

- In what ways might heavy or light rain affect the land differently?

12. Think about what you observed today. What did you learn about the relationship between rainwater flowing on land and how streams might form? Write your answer in your notebook.

13. Clean up, just as you did in Lesson 2.

Ideas to Explore

1. Would you like to do some experiments with runoff? Ask your teacher to make some suggestions.

2. Do you know what time-lapse photography is? You can create your own time-lapse sequence! Ask your teacher to show you how.

3. If your teacher says it's okay, try this experiment: Place a flat rock in the center of your land model and use your sprinkler bottle to rain on the rock. Record your observations. How did the rock affect the results?

4. See what you can find out about rain forests. Where are they located? What happens when it rains there?

Investigating Streams

Think and Wonder

You know about picnic tables, dinner tables, and math tables. But have you ever heard of a stream table? Today, you will build a stream table. Pay close attention to what your stream does to the land.

Materials

For you

    1 science notebook
    1 copy of **Record Sheet 4-A: Comparing Streams**

For you and your group

      Stream table materials
    1 soda bottle of water
    1 cup with small hole (blue dot)
    1 graduated cylinder
    1 black china marker
    1 permanent black marker
      Crayons
    1 piece of string
      Scissors

Find Out for Yourself

1. Think about the model and the rain you created in Lesson 3. Where did the rainwater in your land model go? Share your thoughts with the class. From now on, you will call your land model a "stream table."

2. Pay attention as your teacher shows you the stream table materials. What will you use to model water flowing on land?

3. Read along as your teacher goes over the **Student Instructions for Setting Up a Stream Table Investigation** on pgs. 22–24. Make sure each member of your group knows which step to do.

4. Your teacher will ask one group to demonstrate the instructions. Watch carefully. Remember to keep the stream source cup filled to the marked line.

5. Look and listen as your teacher goes over **Record Sheet 4-A: Comparing Streams.** Today, you will write only in the first column. Remember to use crayons when drawing your results.

6. How might the changes in the land caused by the stream source cup be different from the changes caused by the rainwater in Lesson 3? How might they be similar? Write some predictions in your notebook.

7. With your class, practice using a graduated cylinder. The illustration in Figure 4-1 will help you.

Figure 4-1

Using a graduated cylinder

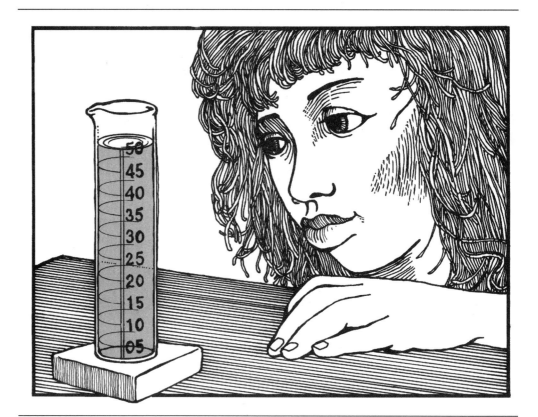

8. Collect your materials and get to work.

9. When you are finished and with your teacher's direction, walk around the room and look at the other groups' results.

10. Share your group's results with the class.

11. What did the water do to the soil in your stream table? Think about these questions:

   ■ How did the water from the stream source change the land? How were these changes in the land different from the changes caused by the rain in Lesson 3? How were they the same? Why? How close were these results to your predictions?

   ■ What did you observe about the particles of sand and gravel in the stream table? What did you observe about the other particles of soil?

- What was the length of your stream? What was the length of your block of soil? Compare the lengths. Are they same? Why or why not?

12. Give your record sheet to your teacher or store it in a safe place in your notebook. You will use it again in Lessons 10 and 13.

13. Clean up. Your teacher will ask one group to do something special with its bucket of runoff. If this is your group, here's what to do:

   - Using a funnel to prevent spilling, pour the runoff from your bucket into the empty "class" soda bottle.

   - Try to leave most of the soil at the bottom of the bucket.

   - Set the bottle aside and cap it. The class will use this bottle of runoff in Lesson 6.

Ideas to Explore

1. Your teacher has added a white substance to your stream table. What do you think it is? Do some research about diatomaceous earth and find out.

2. Lots of songs have the word *water, land, stream,* or *river* in them. What songs can you think of that contain one or more of these words? Make a list.

3. You can use the string from your investigation to measure things that do not have straight lines. Try measuring round or curvy things. What about a river on a map?

Student Instructions for Setting Up a Stream Table Investigation

1. Use the black china marker to write a "4" (the lesson number) on your cylinder. Then label the cylinder with your group letter or color.

2. Place the large pad on top of your work space. Place the small pad on the floor under the edge of the work space. Make sure the absorbent sides of the pads are up.

3. Mix the soil in the stream table.

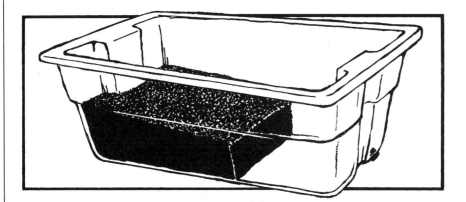

4. Using your plastic spreader, push the soil away from the hole. Bulldoze your soil into a single block that angles slightly up toward the end of the box.

5. Position your stream table on your work space so the end of the box with the drain hole hangs over the edge.

6. Remove the cap from the soda bottle.

7. Attach the Ultra Velcro® on the cup to the Ultra Velcro® on the stream table. Rock the cup back and forth to join the two pieces of Ultra Velcro®. It may feel a little loose and the cup may tilt when filled with water, but this is normal.

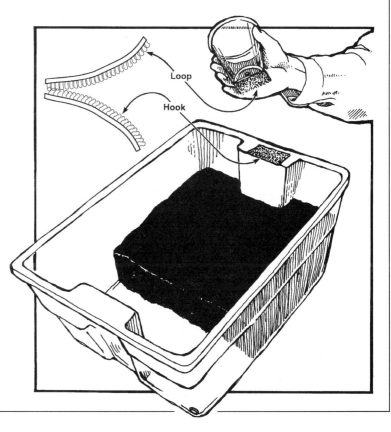

8. When your group is ready, remove the rubber stopper. Hold the bucket directly under the drain hole.

9. Pour the water slowly into the *cup.* Try to keep the water up to the line on the cup at all times. Do not touch the soil once you have started to pour.

10. When you have poured out nearly all the water, collect a sample of runoff. To do this, place the empty cylinder under the drain hole. Fill the cylinder with runoff to the 50-ml mark. Keep the cylinder in a safe place. You will observe it throughout the rest of the unit.

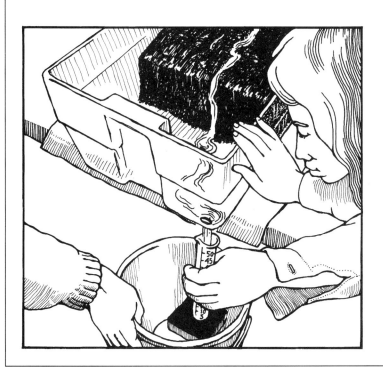

11. Observe and discuss with your group the soil and water in your stream table and cylinder. Record all observations on **Record Sheet 4–A: Comparing Streams.** Do the following steps:

■ On your record sheet describe or draw a picture of your stream. Use crayons and label your picture.

■ Measure the length of your stream. Lay the string along the stream, matching its shape. With a permanent marker, mark the end of the stream on your string. Now remove the string and use a ruler to measure the distance from the end of the string to the mark.

■ Measure the width of your stream.

■ Measure the width of the soil deposited at the end of the stream with a string or ruler.

■ On Record Sheet 4–A, draw a picture of your cylinder of runoff.

Examining Earth Materials

Think and Wonder

The land on earth is made of different **components,** or parts. Let's take a close look at four soil components. They make up the land in your stream table. What do they look like? What happens when they are added to water? How are they different? Let's find out.

Materials

For you

   1 science notebook
   1 copy of **Record Sheet 5-A: Examining Earth Materials**

For you and your group

   1 cup of water
   1 small cup of sand
   1 small cup of gravel
   1 small cup of humus
   1 small cup of clay
   1 spoon
   2 hand lenses
   1 sheet of white paper
   1 section of newspaper
   1 stream table lid

Find Out for Yourself

1. Help the class review what you did in Lessons 3 and 4.

2. Follow along as your teacher goes over the **Student Instructions for Examining Earth Materials** on pgs. 27–28. Do you have any questions? Make sure each group member knows which step to do.

3. Your teacher will pass out **Record Sheet 5-A: Examining Earth Materials.** Pay attention so you will know how to fill it out. Remember that you will want to use lots of "describing" words, or adjectives.

4. One student from each group needs to pick up the materials. Another student should cover the group's work space with newspaper.

5. Now get to work. Talk about what you are doing with your group.

6. Don't forget to clean up! Cleanup directions are on your instruction sheet.

7. What did your group learn about the properties of each soil component? Your teacher will record your thoughts on a "Soil Properties" table.

8. Think about your stream table in Lesson 4. How did the water wear away and drop off gravel, sand, humus, and clay? Talk about this with your class.

9. Look at the lists from Lesson 1. Add any new comments or questions you have about land and water.

Ideas to Explore

1. Ask your teacher if you can set up a classroom observation center. Bring in some interesting things from home to examine and share with your classmates. Use a hand lens to look closely at the objects. What adjectives can you use to describe the properties of each object?

2. Use the steps you used in this lesson to look at a soil sample from your stream table. Look at the sample through a hand lens. Drop the sample in a cup of water. Can you see each of the soil's components in the water?

3. Can you remember a time when you mixed one or more of the soil components with water to make something? Write a story about this experience.

Student Instructions for Examining Earth Materials

Directions: Read all the directions before you begin. You will do each of the following steps four times, once for each of the four soil components, in the order listed on **Record Sheet 5–A: Examining Earth Materials.** Start with gravel. Then test sand, clay, and finally humus. Work as a group. Complete your record sheet as you make observations about each soil component.

1. Pour the gravel onto the sheet of paper.

2. With your hand lens, look closely at the gravel.

3. What do you notice about the appearance of the gravel? How does it look? Discuss your observations with the group. Record your observations on Record Sheet 5–A.

4. Use your fingers to feel the texture of the gravel. Discuss and record your observations.

5. Gently fold your sheet of paper. Using it like a funnel or chute, drop the gravel into the cup of water. Watch it fall. Discuss and record your observations on your record sheet.

6. Stir the water gently with your spoon. Record your observations.

7. Repeat Steps 1 through 6. This time use sand. Record your observations on your record sheet. Use the same cup of water that you used for the gravel.

8. When you are finished testing sand, test clay, then humus. Use the same cup of water each time. Record your observations on the record sheet each time.

9. When you have tested all four soil components, stir the mixture of soil and water again. Record any additional observations on the record sheet.

10. Clean up by doing the following:

- Pour the soil and water from the cups into the rinse bucket. Rinse the cups.

- Return all materials to their original positions on the distribution table.

- Throw away any soiled newspaper. Sponge down and dry your work space.

Where Does the Water Go?
Looking at Ground Water and Runoff

Think and Wonder

What happens when you pour water on different soil components? Where does the water go? How much water will each component hold? After you find the answers to these questions, you will read about your drinking water and where it comes from. How do we use water stored in the ground?

Materials

For you
- 1 science notebook
- 1 copy of **Record Sheet 6-A: Testing Pore Space in Earth Materials**

For you and your group
- 1 small cup of clay
- 1 small cup of humus
- 1 small cup of sand
- 1 small cup of gravel
- 1 cup of water
- 4 graduated cylinders
- 1 chopstick
- 2 hand lenses
- 1 spoon
- 1 set of crayons (orange, black, gold, brown, blue, green)
- 1 piece of white paper
  Newspaper

Find Out for Yourself

1. Think back to Lesson 4. Look at the bottle of runoff that one group collected. How does the amount of water in the bottle compare with the amount of water the group poured on the soil in that lesson? Are the amounts the same or different? Why?

2. Look and listen as your teacher reviews **Record Sheet 6-A: Testing Pore Space in Earth Materials.** Where will you record your predictions?

3. Help your group pick up the materials. Cover your work space with newspaper.

4. Remember to discuss your ideas with your group as you work. Also be sure to use different colored crayons when you draw the soil and water levels in each cylinder. Now start working.

5. Clean up. Here's how:

    ■ Pour the soil-water mixtures from each small cup into the rinse bucket.

    ■ Empty the contents of each cylinder into the lined trash can.

    ■ Rinse the cylinders and cups in the rinse buckets. If necessary, use the chopstick and the bottle brush to help clean the cylinders.

    ■ Return all materials to the distribution center. (Your teacher may ask you to put the four cylinders in your group's storage container.)

6. Share your results with the class. Your teacher will ask some questions to help you discuss your observations.

7. Your teacher will write some words on the board. Explain to the class what you think they might mean.

8. Where do runoff and ground water go after they move over and through the land? Share your ideas with the class.

9. How do we use ground water? Where does your family get its drinking water? Read "Where Does Our Drinking Water Come From?" on pgs. 32–34 and see if you can find out.

Ideas to Explore

1. Do some research on the ground water in your community. How much of your drinking water comes from ground water?

2. What happens when ground water drips in underground caves? Set up an investigation to find out. Use the picture in Figure 6-1 to help you. Then find out more about stalactites and stalagmites.

3. A sponge can hold a lot of water. Can you figure out how much water your soil samples can hold? Ask your teacher to help you.

4. Where does your local water supply come from? How does it get to your house and school? Where does the wastewater go? Write to your water utility company and find out.

Figure 6-1

*Creating
stalactites and
stalagmites*

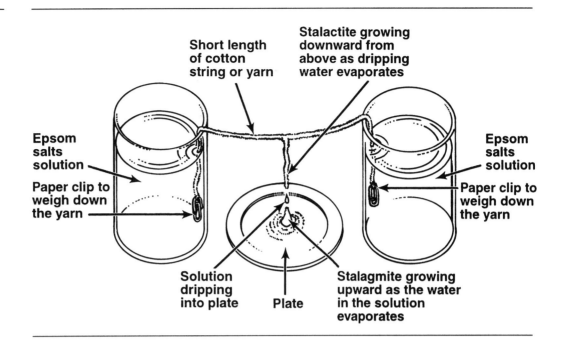

Short length
of cotton
string or yarn

Stalactite growing
downward from
above as dripping
water evaporates

Epsom
salts
solution

Paper clip to
weigh down
the yarn

Epsom
salts
solution

Paper clip to
weigh down
the yarn

Solution
dripping
into plate

Plate

Stalagmite growing
upward as the water
in the solution
evaporates

Reading Selection

Where Does Our Drinking Water Come From?

Have you been keeping track of how much water you use each day? Just think of all the ways you use water. You use it to wash your face after you get up in the morning. At school, you might stop by the water fountain for a cool drink. And there's nothing like a dip in the swimming pool on a hot summer day. You already know that each person in the United States uses an average of 350 liters of water (about 90 gallons) each day!

Most of the water on earth is found in oceans. We can't drink this water. Do you know why? Ocean water is very salty. Set out a pan of salt water in the sun. Over time, the water evaporates and salt is left behind. Scientists can remove salt from ocean water. But this process is expensive and takes a long time.

Our bodies need fresh water. Some fresh water comes from lakes and streams. These sources are called **surface waters.** Other fresh water is hidden underground. **Ground water** is water that has fallen to the earth as rain, snow, or other precipitation. It seeps through layers of sand, gravel, and other earth materials known as **aquifers** (say ah-kwi-ferz). The water stops when it reaches a layer of rock or other hard material. Look at your stream table from underneath. Do you see any water beneath the soil?

How Do We Get Our Water?

If you live in a city or town, you probably get your water from a public utility company. Utility companies pump water to your home either from surface waters or aquifers.

Sometimes utility companies must send the water from lakes or rivers through pipes for hundreds of miles. The pipes that bring water to a big city may be wide enough for you to stand in. In fact, the water tunnels in New York City are so large you could drive a truck through them!

If you live far from the city, you probably get your water from a well drilled in the ground.

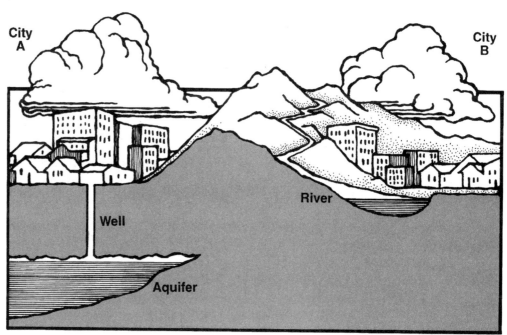

Water sources

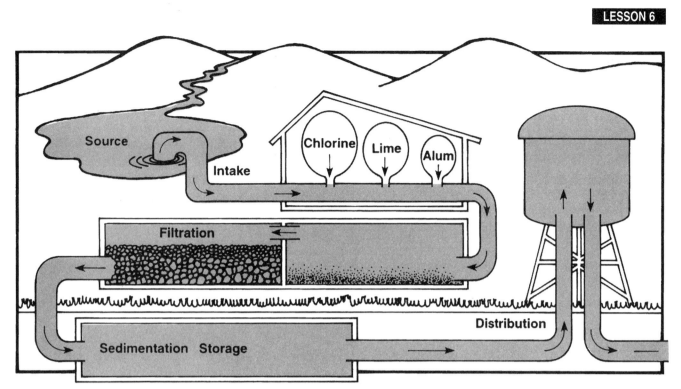

Filtering water at a treatment plant

Well drillers are workers who make holes deep into the earth until they find water. Sometimes a well can be more than 305 m (1,000 ft) deep! After the well is drilled, the driller puts a plastic or steel pipe that looks like a giant drinking straw into the hole. This keeps the soil and rock from caving in. Then the well driller attaches an electric pump to the pipe. The pump forces the water that has seeped into the pipe upward, through the pipe, and into your house.

Cleaning the Water

Have you ever poured sandy water through a strainer at the beach? The strainer is like a **filter.** It separates some of the sand from the water. You might say it helps to clean the water.

The land can be a filter, too. As water seeps through the soil, layers of sand and gravel clean the water. People can usually drink spring water, which has been underground, just the way it is.

Surface waters, however, usually are not clean. Do you remember what the water in your catch bucket looked like? It was very dirty because of sediment. When water flows over land, it wears away soil and rock and carries the particles along. This is called **erosion.** Pollutants—like fertilizer, road salt, and other chemicals—can get into both surface water and ground water. Then the water is not safe to drink.

Utility companies must clean the water before people can use it. In treatment plants, utility companies add certain chemicals to the water. For example, chlorine gets rid of bacteria that might harm you. Alum makes particles clump together and sink to the bottom. This is called **sedimentation.** After the sediment is removed, the water passes through layers of sand and gravel. These layers filter the water and remove smaller particles. This is called **filtration.** Before the water can be stored or distributed to homes and businesses, utility plant workers bubble air through the water to make it taste fresh. Many utility companies add fluoride to the water, too. This helps keep your teeth from getting cavities.

Getting the Clean Water to You

Have you ever noticed a water tower in your town or on top of a building? Utility companies use water towers to store clean water until you are ready to use it.

Why do you think water towers are so tall? Think of pouring water from a cup. The higher you hold the cup, the bigger the splash. That is because the **water pressure** is greater when the water falls from a greater height.

When water is released from the tower, the pressure of the water pushes it down and through pipes. The pipes carry the water directly to your home, offices, and other buildings.

Conserving Our Water

What happens to the water we use after it disappears down the drain? This **wastewater** must be cleaned before we can use it again. Cleaning our water costs money and takes time. Clean water is a limited resource. We must be careful not to waste it. Continue to keep track of how much water you use each day. Then decide if you are using it wisely.

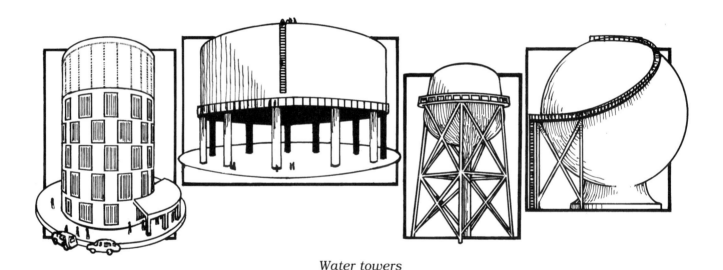

Water towers

Where Does the Soil Go?
Looking at Erosion and Deposition

Think and Wonder

Why is runoff dirty? Where does the soil in your catch bucket come from? Conduct another stream table investigation. Look for places where the water wears away **(erodes)** and drops off **(deposits)** soil. Then you will read about water in another form that also erodes land—glaciers.

Materials

For you

- 1 science notebook
- 1 completed copy of **Record Sheet 5-A: Examining Earth Materials**

For you and your group

- Stream table materials
- 1 capped soda bottle of water
- 1 cup with small hole (blue dot)
- 1 small cup of marine sand
- 7 toothpick flags

Find Out for Yourself

1. Take out **Record Sheet 5-A: Examining Earth Materials.** Look at the questions at the end. When did the water pick up and carry the soil? When did the soil settle to the bottom of the cup?

2. In this lesson, you will look closely at how water erodes and deposits soil. Look and listen as your teacher goes over the **Student Instructions for Tracking the Movement of Soil** on pgs. 37–38. Make certain you understand how to use the toothpick flags.

3. Help your group get its materials and start working. Record your observations and drawings in your notebook. Be sure to show where you placed each flag.

4. Take a look at the other stream tables around the room. Where did each group place its flags?

5. Where was the soil eroded and deposited by the water in your group's stream table? Think about these questions:

   ■ In your investigation, where was the *most* soil worn away (eroded)?

   ■ How would you describe the speed of the water at the time this soil was eroded?

   ■ Where in your stream table was the *most* soil dropped off (deposited)?

   ■ How would you describe the speed of the water at the time this soil was deposited?

   Share your thoughts with the class. Use your stream table to explain your ideas.

6. Why is soil eroded? Why is it deposited? Share your thoughts with the class. Again, use your stream table to explain your ideas.

7. Can you think of some other ways to describe the places in your stream table where soil was eroded or deposited? Discuss your ideas with the class.

8. Clean up. All you need to do is plug the drain hole in your stream table and put your materials away. It is very important not to touch or disturb your land. You will use the stream table just as it is in Lesson 8.

9. What do you know about glaciers? Read "Glaciers: Rivers of Ice" on pgs. 39–40 to learn more. Then record in your notebook one way glaciers erode the land differently from streams.

Ideas to Explore

1. Go on a field trip after a hard rain. See if you can observe where soil has been eroded and deposited by water. Draw and write about your discoveries.

2. Can you figure out the speed of a small, local stream? Your teacher can give you some suggestions on how to do it.

3. Read poems about rivers and streams. One is "Where Go the Boats?" by Robert Louis Stevenson. Illustrate the poems. Then write one of your own.

4. Investigate how glaciers erode and deposit soil. Try moving an ice cube along a pan of soil. What do you observe? Then find out more about glaciers and erosion caused by glaciers. Look on maps. Search for photos of glaciers in magazines and books.

5. Get together with other students. Write a skit or play in which you act out the ways in which water erodes, moves, and deposits soil.

Student Instructions for Tracking the Movement of Soil

1. Bulldoze the land. Attach the cup to the Velcro® on the stream table. Set up your stream table as shown in the illustration.

2. Slowly pour the water into your cup. Try to keep the water at the line. When a stream forms, place a "pinch" of marine sand in the stream near the cup. If the marine sand clumps, break it up gently with the tip of a toothpick.

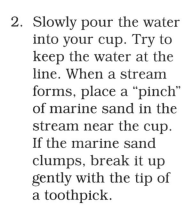

3. Watch the marine sand move.

   ■ Place the flags marked *Slow* in areas where the stream is moving slowly.

   ■ Place the flags marked *Fast* in areas where the water is moving quickly. Stick the flags directly into the soil.

4. Continue to observe the speed of the stream and how soil is worn away (eroded) and dropped off (deposited) by the water. Talk with your group about what you observe.

5. When your bottle of water is empty and your stream is no longer running, look closely at your land.

   ■ Place the flags marked *Wears away soil* in places where soil was eroded by water.

   ■ Place the flag marked *Drops off soil* in one place where soil was deposited by water.

6. In your notebook, draw your stream table results. Label your drawing with the words *Fast, Slow, Wears away soil*, and *Drops off soil*.

7. Record observations in your notebook. Then try to answer the following questions:

   ■ How is the speed of the stream related to the way water erodes or deposits soil? Use evidence from your stream table to support your answer.

   ■ During a heavy rainstorm, what do you think would happen to the soil on a steep hill? Why do you think this would happen?

8. Clean up.

   ■ *Do not* tilt your stream table to drain extra water out of it.

   ■ Put the rubber stopper back in the drain hole.

   ■ *Do not* change the way your land looks. You will draw your stream in Lesson 8.

Reading Selection

Glaciers: Rivers of Ice

Have you ever seen a glacier? **Glaciers** are huge rivers of slowly moving ice that erode the land as they creep downhill. They form in cold, mountainous areas.

To learn more about glaciers, let's take an imaginary helicopter ride. We're heading for the mountains near the coast of Alaska. Fasten your seat belts. The gusty winds may give us a bumpy ride!

We will be flying over a **valley glacier.** This kind of glacier often flows in a V-shaped valley created by a river. On our way there, let's talk about how glaciers form.

Valley glaciers begin when snow collects on the sides of mountains. It never gets warm enough to completely melt the snow. Over the years, new snow falls. It becomes deeper. Sometimes the snow can get as high as two houses stacked together. When this happens, the snow is very heavy.

The weight of the snow presses the bottom layers of snow into ice. The ice crystals lock together. The ice is like rock. It is heavy enough to carve bowl-shaped holes in the sides of a mountain. These holes are called **cirques.**

Over time, the ice spills over the edges of the cirques. The ice begins to flow downhill into the valley below. Usually it moves only a few inches a day. Now the ice can be called a glacier.

Look ahead! Our helicopter has finally arrived at the glacier.

Do you see the sharp mountain peak at the head of the valley? This peak is called a **horn.** A horn forms when there are several cirques around a mountain. The ice in the cirques keeps wearing away at the mountain. The cirques get bigger. The mountain becomes pointed.

Now look at how several valley glaciers are coming together into one gigantic glacier. As the ice moves, it can stick to huge boulders and pull them up from the sides and floor of the valleys. Boulders stuck to the bottom of

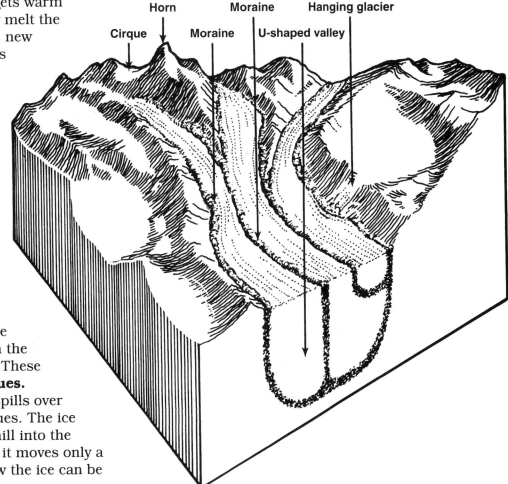

Horn   Moraine   Hanging glacier

Cirque   Moraine   U-shaped valley

the glacier can scour and erode the land. Some of these boulders may be bigger than your classroom. Beneath the ice, the valley is becoming wider and deeper. Now it has a U-shape.

Let's drop our helicopter down and look more closely at the glacier. Do you see the chunks of rock deposited along the sides and front of the glacier? These deposits are called **moraines.** When two glaciers flow beside each other, they both deposit materials. A moraine forms between them.

Have you ever seen ice crack? Glaciers crack, too. Deep cracks in glaciers are called **crevasses.** Sometimes glaciers move over uneven land. The ice on top of the glacier bends and breaks. This is how crevasses form.

Now let's fly east. Can you see a smaller glacier plunging over a steep cliff? It is a **hanging glacier.** It is separate from the main glacier. Huge blocks of ice the size of railroad cars can break off.

Glaciers are always gaining and losing ice. High in the mountains in winter, new snow falls on the head of the glacier. Down lower, it is warmer. The front of the glacier can melt. Sometimes the glacier flows all the way to the sea. Giant blocks of ice break off and crash into the water. That's how **icebergs** form.

It's time to turn our helicopter around. Let's fly back to the coast. As we do, look out your window. Do you see the valleys below? Which one do you think was made by a river? Which one was made by a glacier?

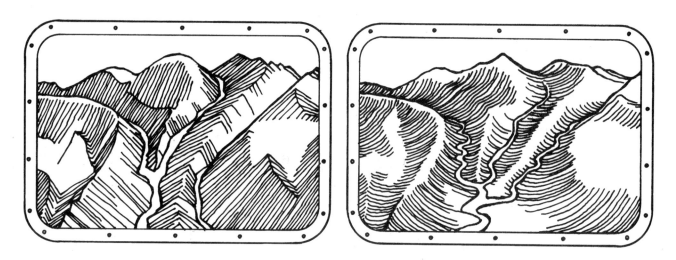

V-shaped and U-shaped valleys through helicopter windows

After you get home, take a look at the land in your own area. Can you tell whether glaciers once flowed there?

Bird's-Eye View: Looking at the Parts of a Stream

Think and Wonder

You have probably heard the term *bird's-eye view*. But what do you think it means? After you find out, you will draw a bird's-eye (or aerial) view of your stream table. Compare your group's aerial view with the others. Are they the same or different?

Materials

For you

  1 science notebook

For you and your group

  Stream table
  3 photo cards (numbered 5, 6, and 7)
  Transparent tape

*Aerial drawing materials for you and your group
  *1 large rubber band
  *1 sheet of plastic
  *1 set of markers
  *2 sheets of white drawing paper
    *Scissors
  *1 large paper clip
  *1 sheet of loose-leaf paper
  *1 permanent black marker

*These materials will be used again in other lessons. In upcoming lessons, you will not see each of these items listed individually. Instead, you will just see the words *aerial drawing materials* in your list.

Find Out for Yourself

1. Look at the aerial photograph on pg. 43. Think about these questions and then share your ideas with the class.

   ■ What do you see in the photograph?

   ■ How do you think the photograph was taken?

- How is this photograph different from pictures you usually take or see?

- How do you think this kind of photograph could be used?

- How is this photograph different from the drawing you made of your stream table in Lesson 7? How is it the same as your drawing?

2. What do you think the term "bird's-eye view" means? Share your ideas with the class.

3. Follow along as your teacher goes over Part A of the **Student Instructions for Making an Aerial Drawing** on pgs. 45–46. Remember, you will not be using water today. Do *not* disturb the results from Lesson 7 while you work today.

4. Help your group pick up its materials and begin working on Part A.

5. Have you finished your aerial drawing? Leave the plastic sheet in place on your stream table.

6. Take a look at some other groups' aerial drawings.

7. Clean up. Here's how:

- Remove the aerial drawing and rubber band from the stream table. Set the aerial drawing aside for now.

- Remove the rubber stopper. Drain any extra water from the stream table into a catch bucket.

- Place the rubber band and set of markers in your group's storage container.

8. You may want to volunteer to tape your group's drawing on the newsprint and describe the drawing to the class. Check with your group to decide who wants to do this.

9. Talk with the class about the ways in which each group made its drawings easier to understand.

10. How are the diagrams alike and different? Which parts of the stream were observed by all the groups? Share your ideas with the class.

11. You may want to volunteer to work on the class drawing of the stream. Check with your group to decide who wants to do this.

12. A volunteer from the class will copy the class diagram from the chalkboard to the newsprint labeled "Parts of a Stream."

13. At a later time, your teacher will return your group's aerial drawing. Listen as your teacher reviews Part B of the student instructions on pg. 46. When it is time, complete Part B.

14. Think about what you have studied so far in the unit. Now look at three new photo cards. Write down the following in your notebook:

- The number on each card

- General observations about each photo card

- Responses to the questions on the back of each card

Figure 8-1

Aerial photograph of the Mississippi Delta, Louisiana, 1983

Courtesy of U.S. Geological Survey

STC / *Land and Water*   Bird's-Eye View: Looking at the Parts of a Stream / **43**

Ideas to Explore

1. Create drawings of different places or objects from a bird's-eye view. This could include the path you take to school or to the park, your bedroom, or a plate of food. Exchange drawings with a friend. Can you figure out what your friend's drawing shows?

2. Bring in maps that show an area from an aerial view. Can you find mountains, lakes, or rivers on the maps?

3. Use the scale on a map to measure distances between certain points.

4. Write a story about an eagle in flight. What can the eagle see from its bird's-eye view?

Student Instructions for Making an Aerial Drawing

Part A: Making an Aerial Drawing

Important: Do not bulldoze or touch your soil during this lesson. Keep your soil as it is. Do not mix the soil.

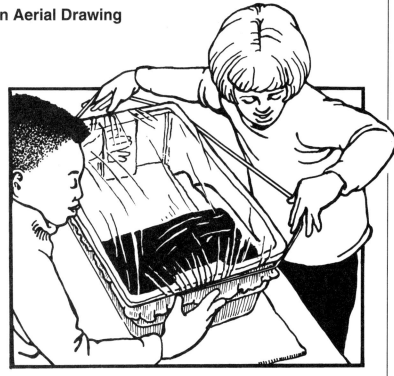

1. Set up your stream table as you have in other lessons, but do not bulldoze, mix, or touch your soil. In this lesson, you will not be running any water through the stream table.

2. Center the piece of plastic over the stream table. Put the rubber band around the stream table to keep the plastic in place.

3. Look down into your stream table. Use your colored markers to draw what you see.

4. Feel free to use color, labels, or symbols in your aerial drawing. Use blue to show your stream and lake.

5. Keep your aerial drawing in place on the stream table so other groups can see it.

6. After all groups have seen your drawing, carefully remove it from the stream table. Drain any extra water from your stream table into your bucket. Clean up as you have in other lessons.

Part B: Preparing the Drawing for the "Big Book of Streams"

1. Tape the aerial drawing to the white drawing paper. You may need to do the following:

   ■ Use scissors to trim the plastic to fit the drawing paper.

   ■ Or wrap the edges of the plastic around the drawing paper.

   ■ Tape the edges of the plastic to the drawing paper.

2. Have one member of your group write a few sentences on loose-leaf paper describing the stream in your aerial drawing. Discuss as a group what you want to write. You might want to record how your land changed, how the stream formed, and the parts of the stream you observed.

3. Tape the loose-leaf paper to a second sheet of drawing paper.

4. Write your group letter or color on both pieces of drawing paper. Paper clip the two pieces together.

Note: You will make more drawings like this one in other lessons. At the end of the unit, your group (or the class) will bind all the drawings together to form a "Big Book of Streams."

When Streams Join: Modeling Tributaries

Think and Wonder

Today, you will do another stream table investigation. This time, the cup will have three holes instead of one. What difference will this make? How will the land look? Find out. Then write about the work you have done so far in the unit.

Materials

For you

    1 science notebook

    1 copy of **Student Self-Assessment A**

For you and your group

      Stream table materials

    1 capped soda bottle of water

    1 cup with three holes

      *Aerial drawing materials

*These are the materials you used in Lesson 8 to create your aerial drawing.

Find Out for Yourself

1. Streams empty into different bodies of water. Try to name some of these bodies of water. Share your ideas with the class.

2. Look and listen as your teacher goes over the student instructions on pg. 49, **When Streams Join: Student Instructions for Modeling Tributaries.**

3. Help your group pick up the materials and get to work.

4. If your teacher says so, walk around and observe other groups' streams while they are flowing.

5. Have one member in your group write a few sentences about the stream pictured in your aerial drawing.

6. Display your group's aerial drawing on the newsprint. You may want to volunteer to describe the drawing to the class.

7. How were the streams alike? How were they different? Before you answer, think about these questions:

   ■ How were the streams that formed today different from those in other lessons?

   ■ What happened when several streams flowed at the same time? Point to evidence in your stream table to support your ideas.

   ■ Look at the soil at the end of the stream. How is it different from earlier lessons? Why?

8. Imagine that your stream table is the Mississippi River drainage basin. Your teacher will ask you to point out some things in your stream table.

9. Attach the aerial drawing and the written description to a piece of white drawing paper.

10. Clean up.

11. You have now done half of the unit. It's a good time to think about your work. What have you learned so far?

12. Pay attention as your teacher goes over the **Student Self-Assessment A.**

13. Fill out your self-assessment.

Ideas to Explore

1. Go on a field trip after a heavy rain. Do you see small streams that come together to make a larger stream? Write about and draw your observations.

2. Look at a map of the United States. Can you find the major drainage basins in North America? What large streams (or rivers) empty into larger rivers? Can you find any landforms created by the rivers?

3. Do some research on the words related to landforms. Where did they come from? What can you find out about the origins of words such as *tributary, rill, delta, head,* and *channel?*

When Streams Join: Student Instructions for Modeling Tributaries

1. Mix and bulldoze your soil into a block, just as you have in other lessons.

2. Set up your stream table. Use the illustration to help you.

3. Attach the clear plastic cup with three holes to the Velcro® on your stream table.

4. Remove the rubber stopper.

5. Place the catch bucket under the drain hole. Make certain you have placed the absorbent pad on the floor beneath the bucket.

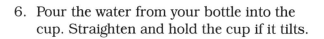

6. Pour the water from your bottle into the cup. Straighten and hold the cup if it tilts.

7. When the bottle is empty, remove the cup. Put the plastic on the stream table. Fasten it with a rubber band.

8. Use your markers. Draw the path of the water. Draw the land. Label your drawing.

Rushing Rivers: Exploring Flow

Think and Wonder

Today, you will model a rushing river. How does the water change the land? Does the flow of water affect how much soil is eroded and deposited? You will also look at more photo cards. What do they tell you about the flow of water?

Materials

For you

1   science notebook
  Record Sheet 4-A: Comparing Streams (from Lesson 4)

For you and your group

  Stream table materials
1   soda bottle of water
1   cup with large hole (red dot)
1   graduated cylinder
1   graduated cylinder of runoff (from Lesson 4)
1   piece of string
1   black china marker
2   photo cards (numbered 8 and 9)
  Crayons

Find Out for Yourself

1. How did you model rain in Lesson 3? How did you model a slow-flowing stream in Lesson 4? How could you model floodwater or a rushing river? Share your ideas with the class.

2. Look at the cup your teacher is holding. It has a red dot and a larger hole than the cup with the blue dot in Lesson 4. What do you think would happen to the land if the water flowed into the stream table at a faster rate?

3. Read along as your teacher goes over the **Student Instructions for Modeling a Rushing Rive**r on pgs. 54–55. Remember that you will need to collect a cylinder of runoff from your stream table.

4. Take out **Record Sheet 4-A: Comparing Streams** (or your teacher will give it to you). Today, you will fill out the column for Lesson 10.

5. Help your group pick up its materials and get to work. When you are about to fill your cup for the last time, be sure to collect a cylinder of runoff. Measure the length of your stream with the piece of string.

6. Take a look at the results of the other groups.

7. How were all of the groups' results the same? How were they different? Think about these questions and share your ideas with the class.

   ■ How did the water in today's stream table change the land? Why do you think this happened?

   ■ How were the changes in the land in today's stream tables different from those in Lesson 4? Compare the length and width of the streams.

   ■ How were the changes in the land the same as in Lesson 4? Why do you think this happened?

8. How does flow affect the way the water erodes and deposits soil? Before you share your thoughts, think about these questions:

   ■ What effect does a large amount of rapidly flowing water have on the amount of soil that is eroded? What evidence in your stream table supports your conclusions?

   ■ Using your record sheet, compare the deltas formed in Lesson 4 and 10. How does the rate of water flow affect the soil that is deposited by a stream? What evidence in your stream table supports your conclusions?

   ■ What situations on earth might cause the flow of water to increase?

9. Compare the cylinder of runoff from this lesson with the one from Lesson 4, as shown in Figure 10-1. How much soil do you think was eroded by the water in this lesson? How might the amount of sediment, or load, from each stream be different? Why?

10. Help your group clean up. Keep your cylinders of runoff for Lesson 13. Give your record sheet to your teacher or store it in a safe place in your notebook.

11. Your teacher will give you two photo cards. In your notebook, write answers to the two questions on the back of each card.

Ideas to Explore

1. Imagine that you are a leaf caught in a fast-flowing stream after a rainstorm. What journey would you take? Suppose you are an ant caught on a leaf. Would you want to be caught in a slow-moving stream or a fast-moving one? Write a story to explain why.

2. The Huang He River in China has flooded over 1,500 times since people began living there. Find out how the animals and people who live there have had to change their lives to cope with the many floods.

3. Look for artwork, photographs, slides, or videos that show slow- and fast-moving water.

Figure 10-1

Comparing loads
of sediment

Student Instructions for Modeling a Rushing River

1. Use the black china marker to write a "10" (the lesson number) on your cylinder. Also write your group letter or color on it.

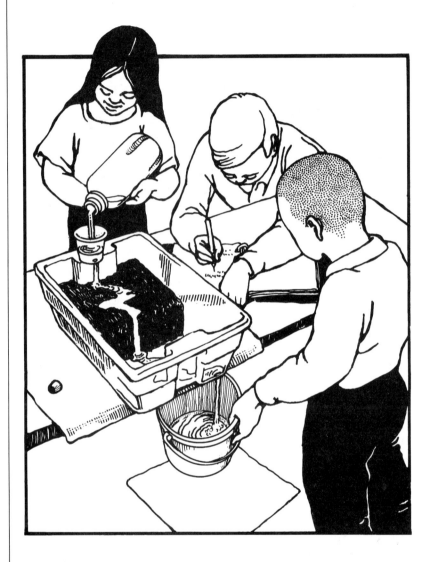

2. Set up your stream table as you have in other lessons.

3. Attach the plastic cup with the large hole (red dot) to the Ultra Velcro® on your stream table.

4. When your group is ready, remove the rubber stopper. Hold the bucket directly under the drain hole.

5. Pour the water slowly into the cup. Try to keep the water at the line on the cup at all times. Do not touch your soil once the water begins to flow.

6. When you have poured out nearly all the water, collect a sample of runoff. To do this, place the empty cylinder under the drain hole. Fill the cylinder with runoff to the 50-ml mark. Keep the cylinder in a safe place to observe throughout the rest of the unit.

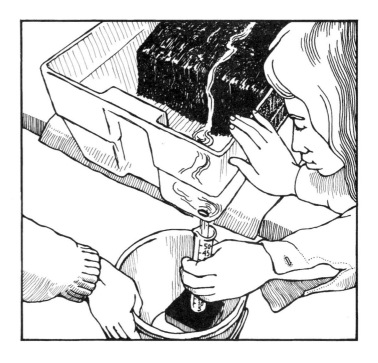

7. Observe and discuss with your group the soil and water in your stream table. Record all observations on **Record Sheet 4–A: Comparing Streams.** Write today's observations in the *Lesson 10* column. Use the string to measure your stream.

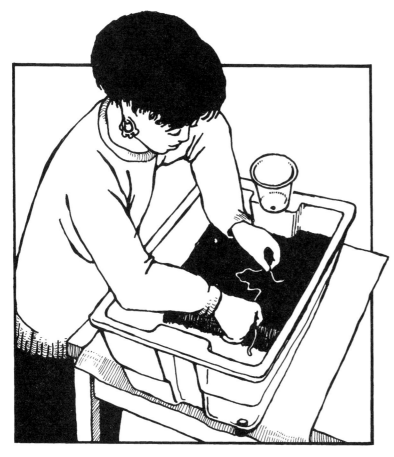

8. Write a description of your stream or draw a picture of it on your record sheet. Use crayons and label your picture.

Hills and Rocks: How Nature Changes the Direction and Flow of Water

Think and Wonder

Until now, you have looked at how water affects land. But what are some ways in which land affects water? How do hills and rocks affect the direction of water? How do they affect the flow of water? Today's investigation will give you some answers.

Materials

For you

    1 science notebook

For you and your group

       Stream table materials

    1 cup with large hole (red dot)

    1 soda bottle of water

    3 paper towels

    3 rocks

    1 small cup of marine sand

Find Out for Yourself

1. What are some ways in which land affects water? Share your ideas with the class.

2. Look and listen while your teacher goes over the **Student Instructions for Testing the Direction and Flow of Water on Land** on pgs. 60–61.

3. Help your group pick up its materials and get to work.

4. Take a look at some of the other groups' streams. What are the results?

5. How are the stream tables alike? How are they different? Discuss your group's results with the class.

6. Look at the drawing you made in your notebook predicting the path of the water. How does it compare with your group's results?

7. Talk with your class about how the rocks and hills affected the flow of water. Think about these questions:

   ■ How did the hills and rocks affect the direction of water? How did they affect the flow of water?

   ■ How was the path of the stream in this lesson different from the path in Lesson 4, where the land was level?

   ■ Did the water affect the hills? If so, how?

8. Now think about the marine sand. How did the speed of the stream change as it flowed near the hills and rocks?

9. Other features on the land, besides rocks and hills, might affect the direction and flow of water. Can you name some? In Lesson 12, you will study one way humans control the flow of water.

10. It's time to clean up. Here's how:

    ■ Remove the rocks from your stream table. Rinse them in the rinse buckets. Put the rocks in your group's storage container.

    ■ Drain the extra water from your stream table.

    ■ Mix the soil.

    ■ Bulldoze the soil with the plastic spreader. Remember to angle the soil slightly.

    ■ Store the stream tables where your teacher tells you to.

    ■ Finish cleaning up. Remember to wash your hands in the rinse bucket.

Ideas to Explore

1. Waterfalls can be beautiful. Do some research on waterfalls. Then ask your teacher if you can make a model of a waterfall in your stream table.

2. Use string to measure the distance of each stream in Figure 11-1. Follow the curves of the stream with the string. Mark the string. Use a ruler to measure from the end to the mark on the string. Write down this distance. Then use a ruler to measure the distance of each stream "as the crow flies." (Your teacher can help you.) Compare the two distances.

3. Research the length of a well-known river. What is the difference between the river's actual length and the distance as the crow flies?

4. Can you find rivers on a map that wind back and forth? Look and see. Do any of the rivers have an oxbow lake, like the one shown in Figure 11-2?

Figure 11-1

Measuring meandering streams "as the crow flies"

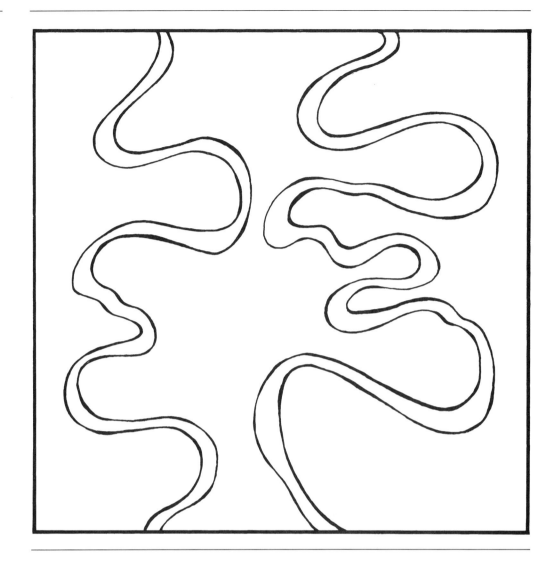

Figure 11-2

Oxbow lakes

Student Instructions for Testing the Direction and Flow of Water on Land

1. Stir your soil. Move two or three large handfuls of soil to the side of the stream table. You will use this soil to make hills.

2. Bulldoze your soil. Use the soil you moved to make one or two hills on the land. Do not make the hills higher than the top of the stream table box. Now put the rocks anywhere on the soil you choose.

3. In your notebook, quickly draw a picture of the land in your stream table as it looks now. Label the rocks and hills. Now make a prediction. What path do you think the water will take? Use a blue crayon to draw your prediction.

4. Set up your stream table investigation just as you did in other lessons. Use the diagram to help you.

- Attach the cup to the stream table.

- Remove the rubber stopper.

- Hold the catch bucket under the drain hole.

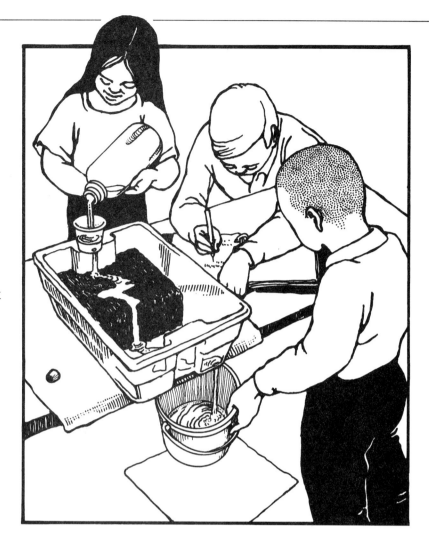

5. Pour the water into the cup. Observe what happens. Sprinkle a few grains of marine sand on the stream. What do you observe about the speed of the stream? Discuss your observations with your group.

6. If your teacher has asked you to create an aerial drawing, place the plastic over your stream table. Use the rubber band to hold it in place. Draw an aerial diagram of your stream table. Label the hills, rocks, and other parts of your stream table. Use color and symbols if you wish. If you were able to observe changes in the speed of the stream, add labels such as *Fast* and *Slow* to your aerial drawing.

Dams: How Humans Change the Direction and Flow of Water

Think and Wonder

Beavers build dams. People do, too. In this lesson, your group will pretend to be a team of design engineers. Your job will be to build a dam. How will your dam affect the direction and flow of the water? Then you will read about a real dam. Why are dams useful? What are the disadvantages of dams?

Materials

For you

   1 science notebook

For you and your group

   1 copy of **Record Sheet 12-A: Building a Dam**
      Stream table materials
   1 cup with large hole (red dot)
   1 soda bottle filled halfway with water
   3 paper towels
  15 craft sticks
  20 toothpicks
   1 cup of gravel
   1 cup of sand
   1 jumbo straw
      Scissors
   6 plastic cubes

Find Out for Yourself

1. How can humans direct the flow of water? What do you know about dams and flooding? Share your thoughts with the class.

2. Imagine that your group is a team of design engineers. Your challenge is to design a dam to help control flooding along the Gaveo River. The Gaveo River is not real; it's imaginary. Now look and listen as your teacher goes over **Record Sheet 12-A: Building a Dam.**

3. Complete steps 1 through 4 on the record sheet.

4. Share your plan with your teacher. Then get your materials. Build and test your dam. You can use any or all of the materials you have been given.

5. Take a look at the other groups' dams. Watch as they demonstrate how their dams work.

6. Think about these questions. Then share your observations with the class.

   - How did your dam affect the direction and flow of water?

   - Did each dam produce the same results? Why or why not?

   - Did the placement of your dam protect your town from flooding? Why or why not?

   - Think about how the rocks and hills affected the direction and flow of water. In what ways were the results with the dam the same? In what ways were they different?

7. Now think about the design of your dam. Which materials worked well for your dam? Which did not? Why? What would you change if you were to design, build, and test your dam again? Share your ideas with the class.

8. It's time to clean up. Here's what to do:

   - Take apart your dam. Remove all plastic cubes, sticks, rocks, straws, and extra gravel from your stream table.

   - Drain any extra water. Put the rubber stopper back in the drain hole from inside the stream table.

   - Rinse the plastic cubes and return them to your group's storage container.

   - Return all materials.

9. Now read "Releasing a River" on pgs. 65–68. When might a dam be useful? What are the disadvantages of dams? After reading the story, write down your thoughts.

Ideas to Explore

1. Imagine you are an animal that lives near a river. Suddenly, the river is dammed and your home is flooded. What will you do? Write down your ideas.

2. Do some research on the Hoover Dam and Aswan High Dam. Debate the advantages and disadvantages of each dam with your classmates.

3. Think of some places in the world that have had major droughts. How have dams in nearby areas helped these places?

4. Draw and label your dam in detail. How did the dam you built differ from your plan? You may also want to research what engineers do when planning and building dams.

Reading Selection

Releasing a River

It is March 26, 1996. A group of scientists stand at the base of the Glen Canyon Dam on the Colorado River. They are looking at the landscape shaped by the river. Earlier in the day, they canoed along the river observing its banks and the organisms—like ambersnails and the southwestern willow flycatcher—that live there.

Millions of years ago, the Colorado River flowed across the Colorado Plateau. The land was high and flat then. Over the centuries, the Colorado River and its floods sculpted and shaped the land until a huge, deep canyon formed—the Grand Canyon.

A Lake Made by Humans

The scientists turn around to look at the massive concrete wall that holds back part of the Colorado River. Behind the dam is Lake Powell. It is the human-made lake, or **reservoir,** that formed when workers built the dam in 1963. Operators of the dam can control the flow of water that passes through the large pipes in the dam and into the canyon.

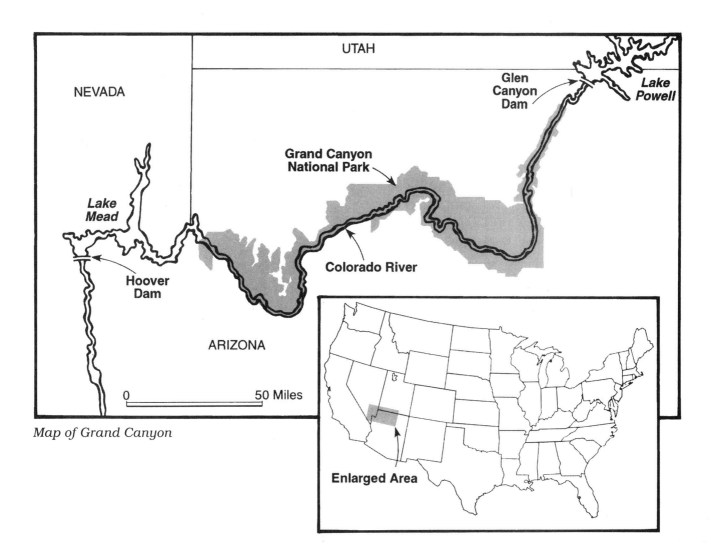

Map of Grand Canyon

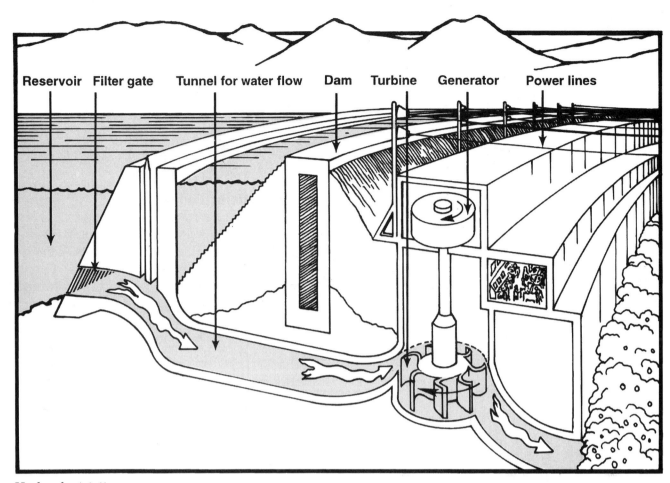

Hydroelectricity

The water stored in the reservoir is used to make electricity. This **hydroelectricity** can provide power to homes and businesses. Just like a waterfall, water from the lake gushes through narrow openings inside the dam. The water hits the blades of **turbines,** or engines, and causes them to spin. These engines power the generators that make electricity.

Towns as far away as 250 miles receive water piped from reservoirs along the Colorado River. Towns can receive water from the reservoirs even during a drought. **Irrigation,** which brings water to farmland through drainage channels, provides farmers with water for growing crops.

People use the reservoir for recreation, too. Swimming, boating, and fishing are only a few of the fun things people enjoy doing on Lake Powell.

Swoosh! The Water Is Released
The dam was built to create electricity. But today, the scientists are going to open the dam. They will create a human-made spring flood.

Swoosh! The dam opens. A thunderous roar echoes through the canyon. More than 117 billion gallons of water blast out of the large tubes at the bottom of the dam. The scientists plan to leave the dam open for a week.

Why would anyone want to flood a canyon on purpose? Before 1963 when the dam was built, the river flooded every spring. The water eroded huge amounts of soil and deposited it along the river's banks. Beaches and sandbars formed when the floodwater pulled back. People on rafting or canoe trips could camp on the beaches. Fish could hide behind the sandbars in the warm, still water and lay their eggs. All along the river, the ecosystem, or environment in which plants, animals, and their environment interact, depended on the floodwater.

When scientists and engineers dammed the river, it no longer flooded each spring like it had for centuries. Across the country, scientists observed that dammed-up rivers were getting smaller. Trees sprouted in the middle of dry riverbeds. Some rivers, like the Colorado, no longer reached the sea. No wonder! Except during extremely high flood years, humans collect and use almost all the water in the entire Colorado River.

What were the scientists' goals for flooding the river? They wanted to restore the beaches along the river's banks. They also hoped the human-made flood would help bring back the natural habitat that plants and animals lost when the river was dammed.

Planning the Human-Made Flood

Scientists carefully planned each step of the flood. They tied transmitters to boulders to study how floods move sediment. They tagged endangered organisms. They even moved snails to higher ground before opening the dam.

And then there was the red water. To measure the speed of the flood, scientists who study water, or hydrologists, at the U.S. Geological Survey dyed the water red. They set up stations along the river below the dam. Each station transmitted data to satellites in the sky. Students, teachers, scientists, and others were asked on the World Wide Web to predict how long it would take the red floodwater to reach each station. Because of computers and satellites, people across the world could follow the flood as it happened!

Using a reservoir

USGS Gaging Stations	Predicted Arrival of Flood	Actual Arrival of Flood (estimated)
Lees Ferry	2 hours, 45 minutes	3 hours
Above Little Colorado River	14 hours, 16 minutes	13 hours
Above Grand Canyon	18 hours, 41 minutes	15 hours
Diamond Creek	40 hours, 39 minutes	37 hours

One person's predictions for the flood

More than a week later, the floodwater reached the Hoover Dam 300 miles away at the lower end of the Grand Canyon. What were the results of releasing the river? It will take a long time to tell how the flood affects plants and animals in the river habitat. But after the dam was closed and the flooding stopped, beaches could be seen along the river. Scientists are calling the flood a success. They might release the river every 10 years.

Humans have learned many ways to control the flow of water. Now they are realizing the effects. What do you think are the benefits of a dam? What are the disadvantages? Should humans release other dammed-up rivers? You might want to do some research to find out more about this topic.

Exploring Slope

Think and Wonder

What will happen when you slope your stream table? How will the direction and flow of water change? How will the slope affect the amount of soil the water erodes? Let's slope our stream tables to find out!

Materials

For you

    1 science notebook

       Record Sheet 4-A: Comparing Streams (from Lessons 4 and 10)

For you and your group

       Stream table materials

    1 cup with large hole (red dot)

    1 soda bottle of water

    1 empty graduated cylinder

    2 graduated cylinders of runoff (from Lessons 4 and 10)

    1 sheet of plastic

    1 large rubber band

    1 small cup of ryegrass seed

    1 small cup of mustard seed

    1 cup of humus

       Books for stacking

       Crayons

    3 paper towels

Find Out for Yourself

1. Today, you will slope your stream table. How do you think it will affect the direction and flow of water? How will the slope affect the way the water erodes and deposits soil?

2. Look and listen as your teacher goes over the **Student Instructions for Exploring Slope** on pgs. 72–73. Be sure to cover your books with an absorbent pad to keep them from getting wet.

3. Take out **Record Sheet 4-A: Comparing Streams** (or your teacher will give it to you). Today you will fill out the column for Lesson 13.

4. Help your group pick up its materials and get to work. The first thing you should do is mark the cylinder with your group letter or color. Then pour the water. Remember to collect one cylinder of runoff from the drain hole when you have almost emptied the bottle of water.

5. Take a look at the other groups' results.

6. Get your group's cylinders of runoff from Lessons 4 and 10. Be careful not to disturb the contents. Then finish the drawings on Record Sheet 4-A.

7. Share your results with the class. Think about these questions:

   ■ In what ways did the water change the sloped land?

   ■ How did the sloped land affect the way the water moved?

   ■ Look at the cylinders of runoff and compare the amount of soil in each one. Are they different? What conclusions can you draw from this evidence?

   ■ How does slope of the land affect the amount of soil the water erodes? What evidence do you have to support your ideas?

8. What are some ways to protect sloped land from erosion? Which soil component might be best for growing plants? Why? Share your thoughts with the class.

9. You need to do some things to get ready for the next lesson. Help your group get one cup of each type of seed, one cup of humus, one plastic sheet, and one rubber band from the distribution center. Then follow these steps:

   ■ Drain the extra water out of the stream table and into the catch bucket.

   ■ Mix the soil with the spoon.

   ■ Bulldoze the soil into a block that is gently sloped, smooth, and approximately 20 cm (8 in) long, as in earlier lessons.

   ■ Sprinkle a mixture of ryegrass and mustard seed over the lower half of the soil near the cliff, as shown in Figure 13-1. Thickly cover the lower half of the soil.

10. Prepare the seeds for germination by doing the following:

   ■ Spread a *thin* layer of humus over the seeds.

   ■ Use a plant mister to water the seeds with a gentle, even spray.

   ■ Place the sheet of plastic over the stream table. Fasten the plastic with a rubber band.

   ■ If possible, store the stream tables in a well-lit area. This will help the plants grow after the seeds germinate and also prevent the growth of mildew.

Figure 13-1

Planting seeds in the stream table

11. Clean up. Use the rinse buckets and bottle brush to clean thoroughly all cylinders. Clean them only after you have made your final observations of this lesson's cylinder. Return all materials to your group storage container or the distribution center.

Ideas to Explore

1. Do you know what contour farming is? Ask your teacher to tell you about an investigation you may want to try.

2. Research the use of contour farming. You can interview a local farmer, write to your state or local soil and water conservation district or farm bureau, or do research at the library.

3. Do research on surface runoff. You may want to write to your state department of transportation. You may also want to ask your teacher about an investigation to try.

4. Ask your teacher if you can use a stopwatch and marine sand to measure the speed of water traveling over slopes of various angles. Then graph your results.

5. Use magazine cut-outs of sloped landscapes to make a picture shaped like a mountain.

Student Instructions for Exploring Slope

1. Mark your empty cylinder with your group letter or color and the lesson number.

2. Stack your books about 18 cm (7 in) high on your work space. Cover the books with the large absorbent pad. Place the smaller pad on the floor.

3. Raise the end of the stream table and set it on the covered books so the stream table is at an angle. Use the illustration to help you. The drain hole should be near the edge of your work space.

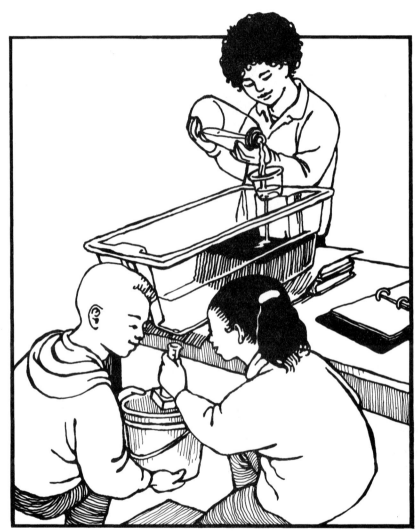

4. Attach the plastic cup with the large hole (red dot) to the stream table.

5. Remove the rubber stopper from the drain hole.

6. Hold the catch bucket under the drain hole.

7. When you are ready, pour water into the cup. You may need to hold the cup steady with your hand. Try to keep the water level with the line on the cup at all times. Do not touch your soil once you have begun to pour.

8. When you have poured almost all the water, collect a sample of runoff. To do this, hold the empty cylinder under the drain hole. Fill the cylinder with runoff to the 50-ml mark. Put the cylinder in a safe place.

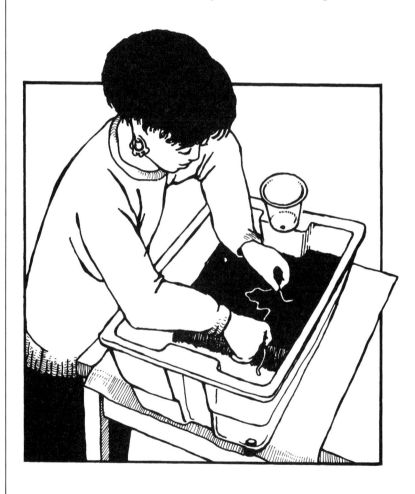

9. Observe and discuss with your group the soil and water in your stream table. Record all observations on **Record Sheet 4–A: Comparing Streams.** Put your observations from today in the *Lesson 13* column. Measure the length of your stream with the string. Use the string or a ruler to measure the width of the soil deposited at the end of the stream.

Plants: Protecting Sloped Land from Erosion

Think and Wonder

In Lesson 13, you planted seeds in your stream table. Today, you will observe the plants that grew from the seeds. How will the plants affect the way that water flows on the sloped land? Do you think removing the plants might affect the land? In what ways?

Materials

For you

   1 science notebook

   1 copy of **Record Sheet 14-A: Investigating the Effects of Plants on Erosion**

For you and your group

      Stream table materials

   1 soda bottle of water

   1 cup with large hole (red dot)

      Books for stacking

   2 empty graduated cylinders

   1 paper towel

Find Out for Yourself

1. Get your hand lenses and your group's stream table. Use the lenses to observe the plant growth. Look at the plants from above, below, and the sides of the stream table. Then share your observations with the class.

2. Today, you will investigate how plants affect the flow of water on land. But first, make some predictions about these questions:

   ■ What do you think will happen in your stream table as water flows across the sloped, plant-covered soil? Why?

   ■ How do you think your results from today's investigation will be different from your results in Lesson 13? Why?

   ■ What do you think would happen if you removed some of the plants before you poured water into the stream table? Why?

3. Look and listen as your teacher goes over the **Student Instructions for Investigating the Effects of Plants on Erosion** on pgs. 77–78. Remember that the investigation has two parts. You will collect a cylinder of runoff after each part.

4. Follow along as your teacher goes over the questions on **Record Sheet 14-A: Investigating the Effects of Plants on Erosion.**

5. Help your group pick up the remaining materials. Before you begin the investigation, remember to mark the two cylinders with your group letter or color.

6. How were your group's results like those of other groups? How were they different? Before you answer, think about these questions:

   ■ What did you observe during each part of the investigation? How were the results of Part B different from those of Part A? How do your results compare with the predictions you made at the beginning of the lesson?

   ■ How did plants affect the way water flowed on the sloped land?

   ■ How did plants affect the way water eroded the soil?

   ■ What happened when you removed the plants from the stream table? Why do you think this occurred?

   ■ What evidence can you point to in your stream table to support your ideas?

7. Now take a look at the two cylinders of runoff you just collected. Think about these questions:

   ■ What do you observe about the contents of the two cylinders?

   ■ Do the amounts of *soil* in each cylinder differ? If so, why?

   ■ Do the amounts of *water* in each cylinder differ? If so, why?

   ■ What conclusions can you make about how plants affect erosion and runoff?

8. Discuss the questions on Record Sheet 14-A with the class.

9. Clean up. Drain the water from your stream table. Put the rubber stopper back in the drain hole. Clean out the cylinders. Return all the materials to the appropriate places. Do *not* remove the plants remaining in your stream table. You will use them again in the next lesson.

Ideas to Explore

1. Look at the "Soil Properties" table from Lesson 5. Set up an investigation to test how plants grow in each soil component. Remember, to make it a fair test, you must keep all things the same (except for the type of soil in each cup).

2. Test some local soil. What are its components? Is it good for growing plants? Why?

3. Think back to Lesson 2. What part do plants play in the water cycle? Take a few blades of ryegrass from your stream table. Place them in a resealable plastic bag. Let it sit overnight. What happens? Find out why.

Student Instructions for Investigating the Effects of Plants on Erosion

Part A: Investigation with Plants

1. Label one of your cylinders "14A" for this part of the investigation.

2. Stack your books about 18 cm (7 in) high on your work space. Cover the books with the large absorbent pad. Place the smaller pad on the floor.

3. Raise the end of the stream table and set it on the covered books as you did in Lesson 13. Use the illustration to help you. The drain hole should be near the edge of your work space.

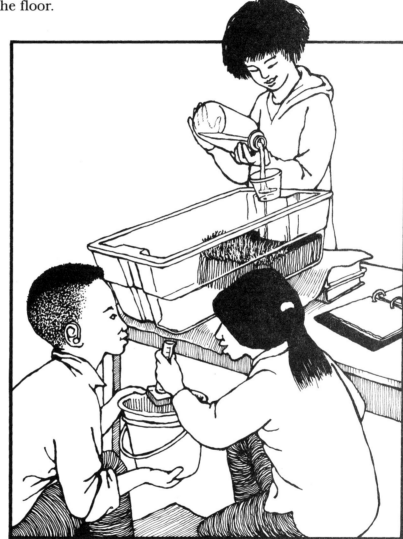

4. Remove the rubber stopper from the drain hole.

5. Attach the plastic cup with the large hole (red dot) to the stream table.

6. Hold the catch bucket under the drain hole.

7. When you are ready, run only *1 liter* of water (one-half of the bottle) through the cup. You may need to hold the cup steady with your hand.

8. When you are almost at the 1-liter mark on your bottle, collect a sample of runoff in the cylinder marked "14A." Fill the cylinder to the 50-ml mark if possible.

Part B: Investigation with Some Plants Removed from the Soil

1. Label the second cylinder "14B" for this part of the investigation.

2. Remove a section of plants from the *middle* of the stream table. Use the illustration to help you. You should be able to see soil where the plants used to be. Place the plants you removed on the paper towel.

3. Pour the water from your bottle into the stream table. Try to keep the water at the line on the cup at all times.

4. When your bottle of water is almost empty, collect another cylinder of runoff in the cylinder marked "14B." Fill it to the 50-ml mark.

5. Now complete **Record Sheet 14–A: Investigating the Effects of Plants on Erosion.**

Planning Our Homesites: Designing and Building a Landscape

Think and Wonder

Do you know what a landscape is? In this lesson, you will plan and build a landscape. What will you put in it? Will it have lots of hills or be mostly flat? Where will you put your house on the landscape? Recall everything you have learned in the unit. What will you do to protect your home from erosion?

Materials

For you

  1   science notebook
  1   plastic cube

For you and your group

  1   copy of **Record Sheet 15-A: Designing and Building a Landscape**
      Stream table materials
      Crayons
  1   paper towel

Find Out for Yourself

1. What do you know about landscapes? Share your ideas with the class. Then tell the class what you think the word *landscape* means.

2. In this lesson, you will plan and build a landscape in your group's stream table. Look and listen as your teacher goes over **Record Sheet 15-A: Designing and Building a Landscape.**

3. Talk to your group about how to complete the record sheet. After you finish the planning part, pick up the materials needed to build your landscape. Remember to choose the materials that fit your plan. You can pick up more materials as you are building, if needed.

4. When your group finishes its landscape, take a look at the landscapes of the other groups.

5. Share your group's landscape, drawing, and predictions with the class.

6. Describe the homesite you chose. Explain why you chose it.

7. It's time to clean up. Carefully place your stream table in its storage area. Use the rinse buckets and paper towels to clean your hands.

Figure 15-1

Sample
distribution
center

Labels visible in figure:
CRAYONS
ROCKS
STRAWS
CRAFT STICKS
TOOTH-PICKS
SCISSORS
PAPER TOWEL
CUPS
GRAVEL
SAND
HUMUS
CLAY

CENTIMETER CUBES
EACH GROUP TAKE 4, EACH A DIFFERENT COLOR

CRAYONS
TAKE 1 SET

TAKE AS NEEDED FOR YOUR PLAN

Ideas to Explore

1. Do some research on how the Grand Canyon formed. How did the Colorado River affect this landscape?

2. Imagine that you are living in the house you put on your landscape. What if a sudden storm comes? Will you be protected? Write a story about the storm and your house. Be sure to describe how the water would flow near the house.

3. Predict how water would flow on your landscape if you "rained" on your land like you did in Lesson 3.

Protecting Our Homesites: Testing the Interactions of Land and Water

Think and Wonder

In the last lesson, you planned and built a landscape. Now it's time to test the effects of flowing water on the landscape. Then your group will make a presentation about what happened. Be sure to explain why you built the landscape as you did. What happened to the homesites? If you were to build your landscape again, what would you do differently?

Materials

For you

1   science notebook

For you and your group

Record Sheet 15-A: Designing and Building a Landscape (from Lesson 15)

Stream table materials

1   soda bottle of water

1   sheet of white drawing paper

Crayons

Find Out for Yourself

1. This is your last stream table investigation. Remember to follow your group's plan. Here's what to do:

- Either slope the stream table with a stack of books or leave it level. Remember to cover the books with the large absorbent pad.

- Choose a cup with a small hole (blue dot), a cup with a large hole (red dot), or a cup with three holes for the stream source.

- Run all but 0.5 liter (500 ml) of water into your stream table. You will use the remaining water to demonstrate the landscape to the class.

- Take notes on the stream path *while it is running.*

- After pouring the water, draw the final landscape on the white drawing paper.

2. Now help your group pick up its materials and begin the investigation.

3. Help your group make its class presentation. Use the remaining water in the bottle to demonstrate how water flows in your landscape. Be sure to discuss these things:

   ■ Why you built the landscape as you did.

   ■ How water affected the homesites.

   ■ The position of the homesites and why you selected those locations.

   ■ Evidence in the stream table that supports how the homesites were affected.

4. Look at your drawing on the record sheet from Lesson 15. How did your predictions compare with your results?

5. Clean up.

6. Write the answers to these questions in your notebook:

   ■ Considering your results, would you still locate your house in the location you originally selected? Why?

   ■ If you were to change your homesite, where would you build your house and why?

   ■ If you were to build your landscape again, what would you do differently?

   ■ What have you noticed about land and water in your community that reminds you of something you studied in this unit? Explain your answer.

   When you are finished writing, share your ideas with the class.

7. Read "Fallingwater: Wright On!" on pgs. 83–85. Why is this homesite unique?

Ideas to Explore

1. Research some of the landforms you modeled in your stream table landscape, such as canyons, valleys, mountains, floodplains, or deltas. How does water affect the development of these landforms in the real world?

2. Make an aerial drawing of your stream table landscape.

Reading Selection

Fallingwater: Wright On!

During the 1920s, Edgar Kaufmann, who owned a large department store in Pittsburgh, Pennsylvania, often took his wife and children to the country for weekend vacations. The family loved to picnic on a sandstone boulder overlooking a 20-foot waterfall on Bear Run. The stream ran through the forest. Mr. Kaufmann dreamed of building a summer cottage at this beautiful site. He wanted to locate his home across from the falls. Could any site be more spectacular?

Yes. How about a home built over the waterfall? A house that straddled the stream? That's what Kaufmann's architect, Frank Lloyd Wright, proposed. Wright even suggested a name for the residence: Fallingwater. "I want you to live with the waterfall, not just look at it," said the architect.

The Kaufmanns were delighted with Wright's idea. And at age 68, the most famous American architect of the twentieth century began to design the Kaufmann's home. First, he did his homework. He studied special maps until he knew the position of every boulder, every tree, and every turn of the stream. Later, Wright visited Bear Run with the Kaufmann family.

Months passed. Still Mr. Wright had not put his pencil to paper. The house had not been designed. Then, as Mr. Kaufmann and several others watched, Wright sketched his plan for the entire four-story house in just a few hours. His design was nearly perfect.

Fallingwater

Fallingwater fits over Bear Run

Construction began on the tree-covered hillside in 1936. The Kaufmanns moved in three years later. In 1963, the Kaufmann family gave the home to the Western Pennsylvania Conservancy. Today, Fallingwater is one of the best-known homes in America. More than 70,000 people tour it every year.

Working *with* Nature

Fallingwater gave Mr. Wright the opportunity to apply an idea he had developed during more than 40 years as an architect. He believed an architect must work with nature, not against it. This approach is called **organic architecture.**

Fallingwater blends perfectly with its surroundings. It is made of sandstone that miners dug from the ground nearby. The house fits over the stream and the surrounding boulders. Some beams are anchored in the boulders. Huge slabs of concrete serve as **cantilevers** to help support the house. They reach boldly over the waterfall and seem to defy gravity. The "backbone" of the house is a large, four-story chimney. From the balcony of the main bedroom, you can look 35 feet straight down into the tumbling waterfall!

Wright did not want the building to disturb local plant life. So he designed a concrete grid that allowed space for the trees on the property to grow. And remember the boulder where the Kaufmanns used to picnic? It's still there—sticking out from the stone floor in front of Fallingwater's main fireplace.

Wright also paid attention to the design and furnishings inside Fallingwater. The ground floor is a large open space that serves as a living room, dining room, and small kitchen. Walls are replaced by windows. Like curtains, they flow from ceiling to floor. The floors are made of natural polished stone. For the doors, Wright ordered special wood from a shipbuilding company. This wood wouldn't be harmed by the moisture. Beds, desks, and dressers are built into the walls. The dresser drawers have straw bottoms so that air can circulate in the moist atmosphere. The shower heads are unusually large. Taking a shower feels like standing under the waterfall!

But Will It Tumble into the Creek?

From the beginning, some people wondered whether Wright's design would work. Was it strong enough to withstand the forces of nature? Today, more than half a century later, it has. Even a tornado that ripped through the area in the 1950s did not damage the house. An ordinary house might not withstand such force. But Wright designed Fallingwater with the landscape in mind. He knew that his special house was adapted to its unusual setting.

The Kaufmann house brought a lot of publicity to Frank Lloyd Wright. Fallingwater has been the subject of magazine stories and has won awards. Some people believe it was Wright's personal favorite. How can they tell? They think he cleverly enclosed his own initials in its name:

FaLLingWater!

Floor plan of Fallingwater